SIGNS & SYMBOLS →

BODY LANGUAGE

RUPERT MATTHEWS

SIGNS & SYMBOLS ➤

Body Language
Codes and Ciphers
Communicating by Signs
Writing and Numbers

First published in 1990 by
Wayland (Publishers) Ltd.
61 Western Road, Hove
East Sussex BN3 1JD, England

© Copyright 1990 Wayland (Publishers) Ltd.

2nd impression 1991

Series Originator: Theodore Rowland-Entwistle
Series Editor: Mike Hirst
Series Designer: Michael Morey

British Library Cataloguing in Publication Data
Matthews, Rupert
   Body language.
   1. Body Language
   I. Title II. Series
   153.6

   ISBN 1–85210–857–6

Typeset by R. Gibbs & N. Taylor, Wayland
Printed and bound in Italy by
L.E.G.O. S.p.A., Vicenza.

CONTENTS

All the words that appear in **bold** are explained in the glossary on page 30.

REFLEX LANGUAGE

How many people have you spoken to today? Ten? Twenty? Perhaps even more than that.

Speech is the means of **communication** that we use most often, but it is not our only way of communicating with other people. All the time, while we are talking and sometimes even when we are silent, we also use our bodies to give out signs and signals. These signs and signals are known as body language.

Most of the time, body language happens without anyone noticing it. People make signs and **gestures**, called reflex signals, without realizing what they are doing.

However, even if we are not always aware of these signals, they are an important kind of communication. If you can work out the meaning of someone's reflex signals, you can understand a lot about their moods and feelings.

The most obvious reflex signals show on the face. If a person is happy they may smile or laugh, whereas if they are angry they may scowl. Although these facial expressions are often made without **conscious** effort, they can become very strong. If a person is embarrassed he or she will flush red, giving a very clear signal. If they are worried, they may look

What can you tell about these people from their body language? Whose body language is friendly? Who is making unfriendly reflex signals?

4

You can tell that this boy is feeling happy from his body language.

pale. The action of crying is another extreme form of reflex signal, showing pain or sadness.

Other reflex signals are not connected to feelings. If you see a group of people sitting down, some may have their legs crossed. People usually cross their legs towards a person they like, but away from someone they dislike. Folded arms have a different function. They act as a kind of barrier, so if a person folds their arms it may mean that they do not like the person to whom they are talking. Another sign to watch out for is someone scratching their nose. Very often, people scratch their noses when they tell a lie or say something about which they are embarrassed.

All these signals are produced unconsciously. Someone seeing these signals may realize that a person is upset or angry, but may not quite be sure why. Next time you are talking to somebody, try to notice their body language. See if you can work out their mood from the gestures they make.

BODY SIGNALS

When people make reflex signals, they do so unconsciously, without thinking about them. But people also use their bodies deliberately to pass on specific messages, as well as to indicate their moods. These body actions are very useful if it is impossible to talk. You may need to make signals if there is a lot of noise, or because you want to communicate with someone who does not speak your language.

You're wanted on the phone.

OK. I've understood.

Where is the phone?

It's over there.

6

Imagine you have a visitor at your home who does not speak your language. The phone rings and the call is for them. How would you get the message across to your visitor? You would probably decide to use body signals.

First you would have to attract your friend's attention. When they look up, you hold an imaginary telephone to your ear and pretend to speak into it. If your friend understands, they might nod or make a thumbs-up sign. They may then look around and shrug their shoulders, to ask, 'Where is the telephone?' You could point with your finger at a door, indicating that the telephone is in the next room.

People use many kinds of different actions to give messages. Waving and pointing are used often, as are nodding and head shaking. Other signals may not be used as often but are easily understood. Placing a finger over the lips is a clear sign for silence, while cupping a hand behind the ear usually means that you cannot hear properly.

Some actions can be understood all over the world. But be careful! Other signals have different meanings in different countries. In places where people speak English, a thumbs-up signal usually means 'OK'. But in other parts of the world it is a rude sign!

If someone makes this body signal, what are they telling you to do?

7

BODY PAINTING

In many cultures, people decorate their bodies with pictures and designs. Sometimes, the human body is painted or coloured with dye which can be washed off later. Other forms of body decoration, such as **tattoos**, are permanent and stay with the wearer for life. Very often, people decorate their bodies for a particular purpose, which is reflected in the types of pattern that they use.

The native people of North America made great use of body painting. When warriors prepared for battle, they would paint themselves with bold designs. They concentrated on their faces which were decorated with red stripes, black masks or white

Above This Maori woman's face is decorated with a traditional pattern of tattoo.

Right This man belongs to a group of Aboriginal people in Australia. Decorated with white markings, he is preparing for a corroboree.

A native American, wearing traditional costume. Can you see how he has painted a design on his face?

circles around the eyes. These designs made the warrior look fierce and aggressive. Other peoples also used war-paint. When the Romans invaded Britain, they found that the Ancient Britons painted themselves with blue paint called **woad** before going into battle.

Body painting can be used for occasions other than battles. The Aboriginal peoples of Australia often decorate their bodies with bold white markings for a corroboree. A corroboree is a special meeting at which men dance and sing.

The Maoris of New Zealand decorated their bodies with tattooing. This permanent form of body decoration indicated the **social status** of an individual. The more important a person was, the more tattoos they had. Some chiefs and kings had their faces covered entirely by tattoos.

9

LANGUAGE IN CLOTHES

Although body painting is now unusual in many cultures, most people still decorate their body in some way – using make-up, jewellery and clothes. Clothes in particular are a kind of body language. People often wear particular styles and fashions in order to give out a message, or to say what kind of person they are.

A T-shirt with a message is a very obvious form of communication in clothing. The T-shirt may carry the name of a pop group, club or organization. This clothing shows the musical taste of the wearer, or tells everyone that they support a particular club. Some people wear T-shirts with the name of a product as a form of advertising.

Sometimes people wear specific clothes for special occasions. If a woman gets married she may wear an expensive wedding dress which is much longer and more elaborate than her normal clothes. The man being married might wear a top hat and a suit with tails, neither of which he would wear in ordinary life. Different cultures and religions have different traditions about wedding clothes. At Christian weddings, it is usual for the bride to wear white. Hindus and Sikhs often wear very brightly coloured clothes.

Do you ever wear a T-shirt with the name of a team that you support?

A Hindu bride preparing for her wedding. Because it is a happy event, she is wearing brightly coloured clothes, and has a garland of flowers.

A Chinese bride may wear an outfit decorated with embroidered dragons and phoenix, which are signs of good luck.

All these special clothes show that the couple consider marriage to be a joyful and special event. When attending funerals, people in many different cultures normally wear dark clothes, sometimes with a black tie or armband. Black is a sign of a sorrowful mood.

Clowns wear clothes which make them look funny. Every clown has his own special outfit and style of make-up, which no other clown may use.

ANIMAL BODIES

Humans decorate their bodies for a purpose, but the natural decoration of animals may have a special meaning too. Over hundreds of thousands of years, the bodies of animals have **evolved** certain colours and patterns. These decorations give out signals or

This poison frog lives in the rain forests of Costa Rica in Central America. Its bright orange body and blue legs stand out against the green leaves of the forest.

messages from one animal to another. Very often, a creature's colouring is a way of defending itself from **predators**.

Several types of small, brightly coloured frogs live in the rain forests of South America. These creatures are boldly patterned with yellow, red, blue and green, which makes them easy to see. Most creatures have **camouflaged** bodies and try to hide from their enemies, but these frogs actually want to be seen by hunters. The

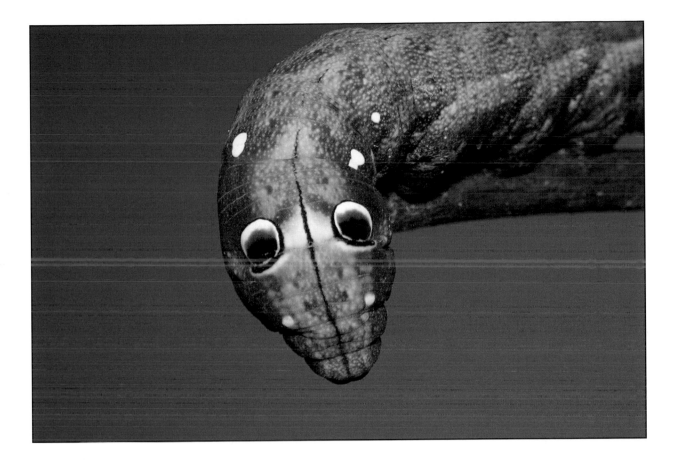

bright skin contains poison glands. Any predator which ate one of these frogs would become extremely ill. The hunters have therefore learnt to avoid eating bright-coloured frogs.

Other creatures have similar body markings which frighten away their enemies. The flower mantis is an insect which lives in tropical forests. Most of the time, it is cleverly camouflaged to look like a flower. However, the mantis also has wings patterned with eyespots, which make it look much bigger and fiercer than it really is. The flower mantis can open its wings suddenly, hissing as it does so, to

Like the American swallowtail caterpillar, this hawkmoth larva tricks its predators into thinking that it is a snake.

scare away any approaching birds. An animal which can frighten a predator in this way, by suddenly showing a patch of bright colour, is said to have 'flash coloration'.

The American swallowtail caterpillar has an even more cunning way of tricking its enemies. It has large spots, like staring eyes, on its body. When it is disturbed, it shows these spots so that its predators will think that it is a snake.

ANIMAL MATING SIGNALS

Mating happens when two animals, a male and a female, join together to produce young. Body language is a very important part of mating. Different body decorations and body signals are the way in which animals attract a mate.

Many birds have bright, colourful **plumage** to attract a mating partner. Peacocks have beautiful, long tail feathers, which they fan out to impress the female birds. By showing off his handsome body, the male bird is telling the female that he is strong and well-fed, and that he is likely to be the father of healthy chicks.

Like the peacock, the male frigate bird also shows off part of his body. The bird has a pouch of red skin hanging from his throat. When he is ready to mate, he blows the pouch into a huge red balloon filled with air.

Some animals use graceful movements to attract a mate. Stickleback fish, which live in freshwater ponds, do a kind of dance. First the male fish makes a nest of pondweed at the bottom of the pond. Then he looks out for a female, and when he finds one, dances towards her in a zigzag pattern. If the female fish is

The peacock uses its brightly coloured tail to attract a mate.

Left *The male frigate bird, puffing up his bright red pouch to attract a female.*

Below *A male stickleback, showing a female fish the way to his nest.*

attracted, she will swim towards the male, and eventually follow him down to the nest.

The great-crested grebe, a bird which lives near lakes, also performs a mating dance. Both males and females move their bodies in many different ways, and before a couple can mate, the birds go through an elaborate mating **ritual**. As part of this ritual, the birds shake their heads at one another and stand up in the water, holding waterweed in their beaks.

ANIMAL COMMUNICATION

Although body language is an important part of animal mating rituals, it is a vital means of communication in many other situations too. Many animals have greeting rituals. When different members of the same **species** meet in the wild, they may be uncertain whether they are facing an enemy or a friend. So they go through careful greeting rituals to make sure that the other animal does not intend to attack.

Other animals make special signals to warn the members of their species if there is danger nearby. One kind of deer in North America has a white tail. When it is frightened, it runs away with its white tail held upright in the air. The other deer see this warning sign and know to run away too.

Honey bees also use body signals to pass on information. They spend the summer collecting **pollen** and **nectar** from flowers to

Two African lions greeting one another.

make honey. During the winter, this honey will provide them with food. If a bee finds a large group of flowers, it returns to the hive. There it 'dances', flying around in a figure of eight, wriggling and shaking its body as it does so. When the other bees see these movements, they learn where the flowers are and fly out to harvest the pollen.

Like humans, animals also express their moods and feelings through facial expressions. Chimpanzees open their mouths wide and show their teeth when they are frightened or excited. They often pout as a sign of greeting, and press their lips together and jut out their jaws when they want to look threatening.

Above A North American whitetail deer. It holds its white tail up in the air as it runs, to warn other deer of the presence of danger.

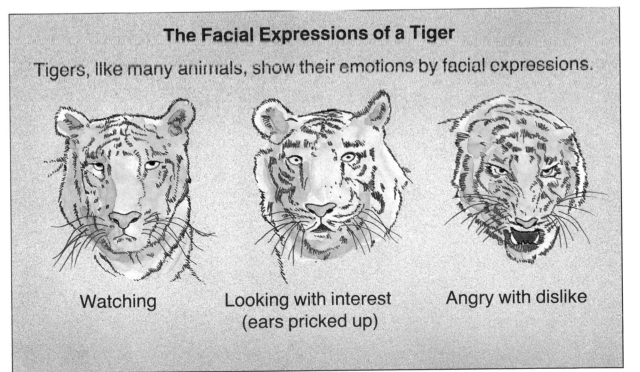

The Facial Expressions of a Tiger

Tigers, like many animals, show their emotions by facial expressions.

| Watching | Looking with interest (ears pricked up) | Angry with dislike |

MIME

In the theatre, body language has developed into a special art form, called mime. Mime artists are actors who do not use their voices. They entertain an audience and tell a story just by different movements of the body.

In the simplest mimes, a person pretends to do an action, such as digging, without actually doing it. In the theatre these simple mimes have been refined and improved so that the mimer creates the impression that they are handling objects which are not really there. They will pretend to run their fingers over imaginary objects, to pick them up and to use them.

Skilled mimers can 'use' imaginary tools to work on imaginary objects. Or they can pretend that they are enclosed in

CHARADES

Charades is a good game for a small group of people. You can play it to practise and develop your miming skills.

First, one person chooses the title of a well-known book, play or television programme. Then, they have to stand in front of their friends and, without speaking, perform a mime, or charade, which suggests the title they have chosen. To make the charade easier, you can mime separately each of the different words that makes up the title.

When someone guesses the title correctly, they take the next turn to perform a charade.

Marcel Marceau performing a mime. He is one of the most famous mime artists in the world.

an invisible box. If the actor is very good, the audience almost believes that the invisible objects are real. One of the most important miming skills is to remember where imaginary objects are supposed to be. The audience would lose interest if a mimer walked through a place where he was pretending a wall existed.

19

POPULAR DANCE

Dancing is one of the oldest kinds of entertainment. We have evidence that as long ago as Ancient Egyptian times, people moved their bodies in time to music. Over the centuries, most cultures have developed some style of folk dancing.

Folk dancing is closely linked to the traditional life styles of local groups of people, and many dances contain body language with its own special meanings.

In Scotland, people still perform the traditional sword dance. It displays the agility of the dancer and also reflects the warlike character of the ancient Highland clans. The Cossack sabre dance, performed by men from the southern part of the USSR, is even more violent. In this dance men carry long swords and strike them against each other in time to the music. They also display their great strength by doing high kicks and leaps.

In some cultures, dance can have a religious meaning. The native people of North America

Girls performing the sword dance at a dancing competition in Scotland.

Right Breakdancing is a way for someone to show how athletic they are.

Below Dancing can often form part of a religious ceremony. This woman is a priestess of the Condomblé religion in Brazil, dancing for the god, Yansã.

perform special dances which are prayers to the gods. In one folk dance, the dancers pray for a successful bear hunt. Someone wears a bear skin and pretends to be a bear. The other dancers threaten the bear with spears and at the end of the dance they mime out the act of killing it.

A popular type of modern dance is disco. At a disco, people can make up their own steps as they go along. A disco is a good place to look out for body language. Each of the dancers is putting on a show. The way in which someone dances expresses their mood and their reaction to the music.

STORIES IN DANCE

Although many people enjoy dancing themselves, dance is often performed as an entertainment before an audience. Many cultures throughout the world have developed classical forms of dance, in which the dancers perform a complex dance routine, which tells a story.

In India, an ancient style of dance called Bharat Natyam is very popular. The dance is performed by a solo woman performer, accompanied by a small band of musicians. For part of her performance, the dancer will

A Bharat Natyam dancer. Even her eye and finger movements have special meanings, so that she can tell a complicated story through her dance routine.

MAKE UP A DANCE ROUTINE

You can make up your own dance routine to tell a story or express your feelings about a piece of music.

First, choose a piece of music you like. Then listen to it. Close your eyes and let the music suggest a scene or a story to you. Then work out a few simple movements to express what you are thinking. Your routine does not need to be very complicated. The most important thing is to perform the correct movement at the right time and to put across your feelings about the music.

If you like, you can work out a number of different dance routines, one each to a different kind of music.

act out a popular Hindu religious story, such as that about the birth of the god Krishna. She tells the story using arm and hand movements, and by showing different emotions on her face.

Classical ballet, too, is often based on a story. This style of dancing first developed in France and Italy about three hundred and fifty years ago. By the nineteenth century, ballet performances were common throughout Europe. Many composers began to write music specially for the ballet, and through the actions of the dancers on stage and the emotions expressed in the music, the audience could follow the thread of even quite complicated stories.

One of the most famous of all ballet composers was the Russian, Tchaikovsky. He wrote *The Nutcracker*, *The Sleeping Beauty* and *Swan Lake*, all of which are still very popular today.

SPECIAL SIGNALS

Some types of body language form part of a special code. In this kind of body language, different body movements have very specific meanings. Often, body signs are used to give instructions.

Police officers sometimes use hand signals to control traffic. They need to give exact instructions to drivers who can not hear spoken commands. By using hand movements, police officers can tell a driver to stop, to advance, to turn left or right or to reverse. All drivers must know and recognize these traffic signals.

Orchestra conductors also need to give instructions to their players, but they cannot talk as they would interrupt the music. Instead, conductors use their arms. With one hand they may beat the time of the music. The steady, rhythmic movements of the beating hand help the players to keep in time with each other. The conductor also uses his hands to give other instructions. He may point at a section of the orchestra when it should begin playing. He can tell the orchestra to play more quietly by placing his finger to his lips, or make it play more loudly by pushing his arm up.

At racecourses you can see a special kind of body language called bookies' tic-tac. Bookies are bookmakers, people who take bets on horse racing. At a race meeting, they use hand signals to tell one another how the betting is going and to find out which horse is favourite to win the next race.

Another type of formal body signal are the salutes which members of the armed forces

A bookmaker at a racecourse. She uses a system of body signals called bookies' tic-tac to say which horses are favourites to win.

Left Police officers use a system of body signals to direct traffic.

Below Orchestral conductors use body language to communicate with their players.

make when they greet each other. The most usual salute is to raise the hand to the forehead. The United States armed forces salute with the palm of the hand facing down, but the British Army and Air Force salute with the palm facing forward. However, both of these salutes have the same origin. They come from the action made in medieval times by knights, who raised the visors, or face masks, of their helmets to show their faces when they met.

SPORTING SIGNALS

In some sports, members of a team need to communicate. Yet very often they cannot speak to each other because they are too far apart, or the noise from the crowd of spectators drowns out their voices. In these cases, body language becomes an important part of the sport.

In baseball, the pitcher and the catcher communicate by hand signals. The pitcher needs to tell the catcher what kind of ball he will throw, without the batter, who is on the opposing team, finding out. The catcher stands behind the batter, and makes different signs, which stand for different kinds of ball. When he makes the sign for the next ball, the pitcher nods, and the catcher knows what to expect. But the batter can not see these hand signals, and so he can not predict how to hit the ball.

In baseball, the catcher, who crouches behind the batter, uses hand signals to tell the pitcher how to throw the ball.

The Body Signals of an American Football Referee

In American football, the referee uses body signals to explain what is happening on the pitch to the scorers and crowd. These are just four of the many signals he needs to know.

Illegal use of the hands.

Player out of bounds when catching a pass.

Tripping - a foul caused when one player tries to trip up another.

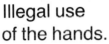

Time - out
a signal which tells
the time - keeper to stop the
official running clock, because
there is a break in play.

In soccer too, hand signals are common. When a player without the ball sees a chance to score, he signals to the player with the ball. He waves to gain attention and then points to show where the ball should be kicked.

In other sports there are more complicated body signalling systems, used by referees and **umpires**. The officials use body movements to give instructions to the players and to tell the spectators and scorers what has happened. To understand games like American football or cricket, you need to know the meanings of all the different signals.

27

RELIGIOUS GESTURES

In many religions, certain body movements can have a special significance.Often people may perform **symbolic** actions as part of a ritual or ceremony. Other body signals emphasize the beliefs that a person holds.

Some Christians make the sign of a cross when they say a prayer. The cross is an important sign, because it reminds people of the crucifixion of Christ, which is a central part of Christian belief. Other actions have become an

Christians often kneel to pray. This woman is also using a string of rosary beads, to count the prayers that she is saying.

important part of Christian ceremony. Some Christians kneel, clasp their hands together and close their eyes when they pray in church. For other Christians, it is traditional to sit down, stand up, or even to raise their arms during prayer.

Muslims also have body language attached to prayer. They pray at particular times of the day, every day. When prayer time approaches, Muslims should kneel on the ground facing towards the holy city of Mecca. They then bend forward so that their foreheads touch the ground, while **reciting** prayers. This action is repeated

A group of Muslims outside a mosque. When they pray towards Mecca, Muslims are showing respect for their holy city, which was the home of the prophet Muhammad.

several times until all the prayers have been said.

When Hindus pray, they usually do so in front of a **shrine**, either in a temple or in their own home. It is normal for them to stand or kneel before the shrine, and then to salute the god by putting both hands together in the traditional Hindu greeting. In some temples, you may also see people walking in a circle around a shrine.

GLOSSARY

Camouflage   A kind of disguise that makes something difficult to see against its surroundings.

Communication   The act of passing on, or sharing, thoughts, ideas and information.

Conscious   Aware of what you are doing or what is happening around you.

Evolve   To develop gradually.

Gestures   Movements or signals made with a part of the body.

Nectar   A sweet liquid produced by plants.

Plumage   Feathers.

Pollen   The yellowish seed dust found inside flowers.

Predator   A hunter.

Recite   To say out loud.

Ritual   A fixed set of actions that are often repeated.

Shrine   A sacred or holy place.

Social status   A person's importance and influence within a community.

Species   One of the groups into which all plants and animals are divided.

Symbolic   Standing for, or meaning, something else.

Tattoo   A permanent form of body decoration. Tattoos are made by pricking a person's skin with needles, and then staining it with colours.

Umpire   The person at a cricket or tennis match who makes sure that the game is played according to the rules.

Woad   A blue vegetable dye, used for body painting by the Ancient Britons.

BOOKS TO READ

Animal Signals by Malcolm Penny
  (Wayland, 1989)
Ballet Company by Kate Castle
  (Franklin Watts, 1984)
Dance by Eleanor van Zandt
  (Wayland, 1988)
People and Customs, Lynda
  Snowdon (advisor)
    (Macmillan, 1985)
Theatre by Howard Coxton
  (Wayland, 1989)

PICTURE ACKNOWLEDGEMENTS

Allsport cover, 24; Barnaby's Picture Library 8 (above); Cephas 5, 28; Oxford
Scientific Films 12, 13, 14, 15 (both), 16, 17; Paul Seheult 4,6 (all), 7, 11, 18, 23;
Topham Picture Library 8 (below), 19, 21 (right), 22, 26; Wayland Picture Library 21
(left); Zefa 9, 11(both), 20, 25 (both), 29. All artwork is by Stephen Wheele.

INDEX